questions and answers about Seashore Life

by ILKA KATHERINE LIST

woodcuts by the author/line drawings by ARABELLE WHEATLEY

FOUR WINDS PRESS / NEW YORK

PUBLISHED BY FOUR WINDS PRESS
A DIVISION OF SCHOLASTIC MAGAZINES, INC., NEW YORK, N.Y.
COPYRIGHT © 1970 BY ILKA KATHERINE LIST
ALL RIGHTS RESERVED
PRINTED IN THE UNITED STATES OF AMERICA
LIBRARY OF CONGRESS CATALOGUE CARD NUMBER: 71-105340

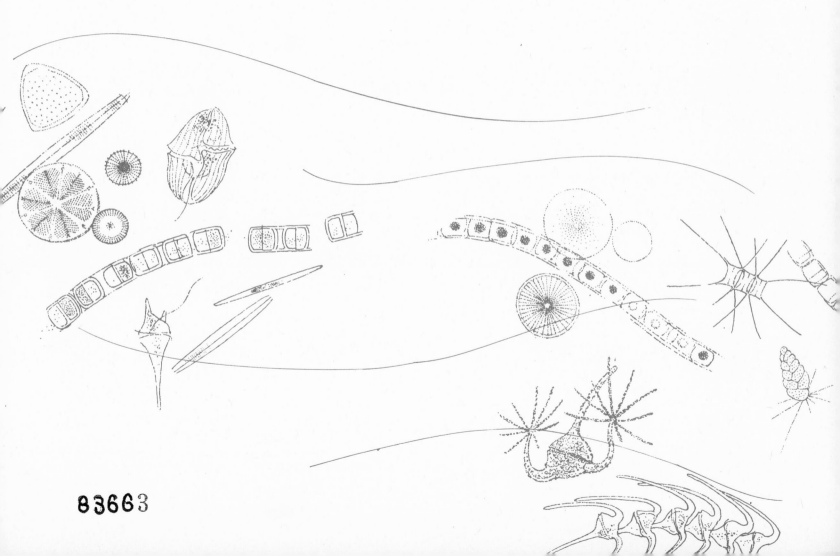

To Lee, Jonah, and Natasha

CONTENTS

questions and answers about **Seashore Life**

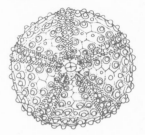

INTRODUCTION

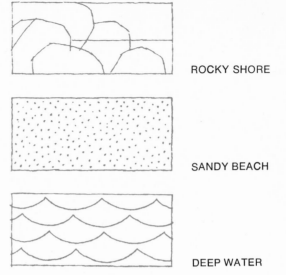

ROCKY SHORE

SANDY BEACH

DEEP WATER

What kind of animals are in this book?

All of the animals in this book are seashore animals without backbones. All of them live in the ocean and all, almost without exception, will die if kept out of it too long. Except for one kind of periwinkle that has almost developed lungs, the animals in this book breathe, eat, grow, and reproduce in the sea. When they are young, most of them drift in the changing tides, developing from eggs into animals that are ready for life on the shore.

Some of them take up life on the rocky shore. They are found exposed on rocks, hidden under seaweed, and deep in tide pools. In this book, these animals are marked with a

Others can live only on or under sand or mud. These animals are marked with a

And a few live in water too deep for us to explore. These animals are marked with a

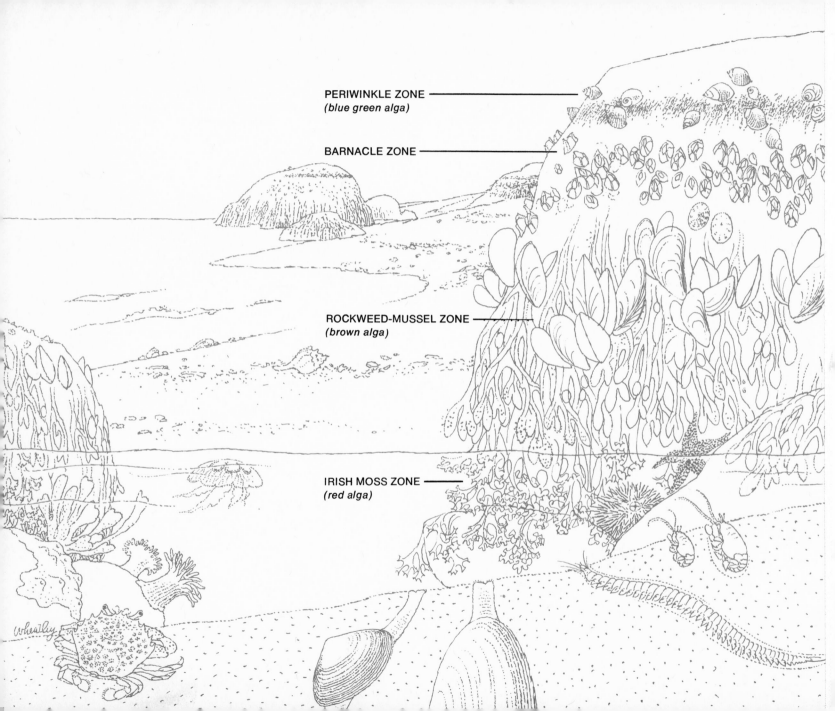

PERIWINKLE ZONE
(blue green alga)

BARNACLE ZONE

ROCKWEED-MUSSEL ZONE
(brown alga)

IRISH MOSS ZONE
(red alga)

Where do you find animals on the rocky shore?

On a rocky shore, certain animals live in certain places. These places are called zones, and each one is a little different from the others. In one zone, near the edge of low tide, the rocks are almost always under water. In another zone, close to land, the rocks are almost never covered by the sea. Splashing waves fill the little pools there, and the temperature goes high in summer and very low in winter. Down where the rocks are usually under water the temperature is more steady. Animals living there do not have to get used to as many changes. Usually animals that live well in one zone cannot live well in a different zone.

Do rock animals notice changes in the weather and the tides?

Animals living on rocks that lie uncovered at low tide have some way of sheltering themselves or protecting their soft parts from the drying air. Some of them pull themselves into shells. Others close up and stay that way for a few hours. All of them can wait for the tide to come back.

Most rock animals can stand a good bit of warming up and cooling down without dying. Their bodies have adapted to the kinds of changes they meet on the rocks. If they find their tide pool made fresh by a sudden rainfall, or too cold or too hot, they depend on the returning sea to bring things back to normal.

15

Where do you find sea animals on a sandy beach?

On a sandy beach with surf, sea animals dig down under the sand. They find protection from the waves there, and cannot be pushed up onto the dry sand.

On a sandy beach that has no surf, some of the animals, such as clams and moon snails, are under the sand. Some, such as hermit crabs and dog whelks, creep along the top of the sand.

Are there any animals on a stony beach?

On a beach made of small stones that can roll around and knock together, you won't find any animals. There is nothing they can dig into, and it is too easy for them to get smashed between rocks.

16

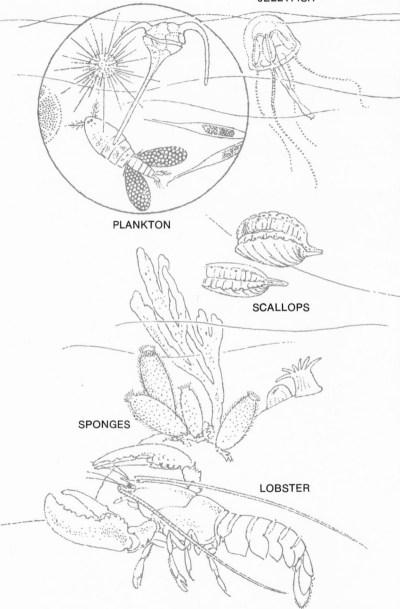

JELLYFISH

PLANKTON

SCALLOPS

SPONGES

LOBSTER

Do beach animals notice the tides?

All of the beach animals that live near the edge of the tide adapt to its changes. When the tide is out, some burrow deeper to stay cool and keep from drying out. Others follow the water up and down the beach, finding new places to dig as the tide changes.

What deep-water animals can you see?

In the fall, you can see jellyfish swimming near the beach. Lobsters live too far out, but when they are brought into the fish markets you can see them there. It's harder to see a living scallop, for only a scallop's muscle finds its way into fish stores. Usually we must be satisfied with pictures in books and magazines.

But the hardest thing of all to get a chance to study is plankton, the microscopic plants and animals that drift in the currents of the sea. Plankton must be gathered in special nets from the surface waters of the ocean and viewed under a microscope.

17

SPINY-SKINNED CREATURES

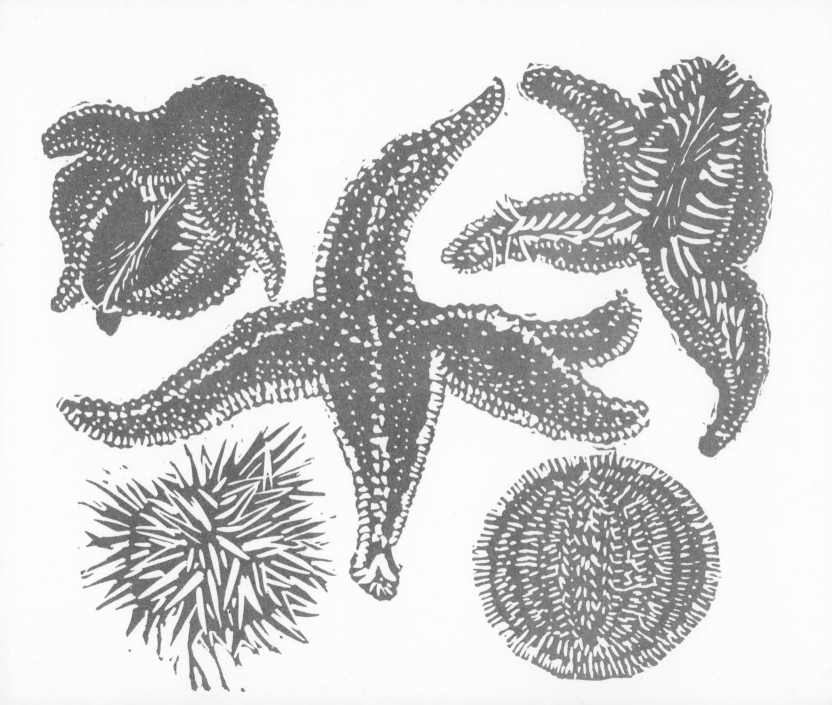

Sea Urchins

What do you call this gray-green ball of spines?

If you have found a spiny ball hiding inside a crack or deep under water and seaweed, you have found a sea urchin. In the cool waters of northern seas, the spines on the urchin can be a little sharp, but they are not dangerous. But in the warm waters of the tropic sea, the spines on the urchin are deadly poison. Scientists do not know for sure why the tropical urchin has poison spines, and the northern one does not.

You can hold the northern urchin in your hand and take a close look. Tucked in between the spines are five rows of tube feet, and on the bottom of the ball is a small, round hole with the tips of five teeth sticking out of it. All of the urchin's most important parts are divided among five sections. This is true of the starfish also, and that is a way that you can tell they are relatives.

Can a sea urchin see me?

Urchins use the sense cells on their skin to feel and taste things in the water. They have no eyes to see with. The most an urchin can do is to sense the light and dark with certain sensitive places of his body. Seeing needs an eye and a brain, and an urchin has neither.

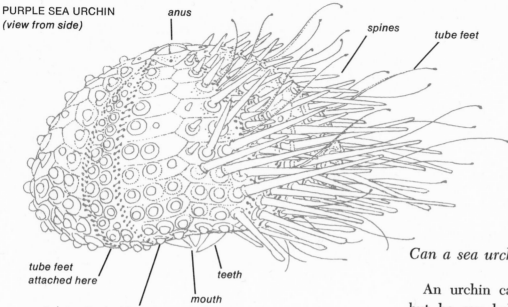

PURPLE SEA URCHIN
(view from side)

anus

spines

tube feet

tube feet
attached here

spines attached here

mouth

teeth

Can a sea urchin go anywhere?

An urchin cannot leave the sea without dying, but he can hobble across the rocks under water. A sea urchin uses his teeth and bottom-most spines as stilts. His teeth are large, but we can see only a small part of them. Many rods and muscles on the inside of the urchin move the teeth in and out. Other muscles move the spines. He grips the rock with his tube feet, and shoves himself along with his teeth. As he moves, his teeth scrape tiny plants off the rocks for food.

A sea urchin's skeleton is not on the outside of his body although it may seem to be. It is on the inside as ours is. But an urchin's skin is very thin, and in some places it wears away altogether, letting the skeleton come through. That is why an urchin's skeleton looks as though it is on the outside of his body.

22

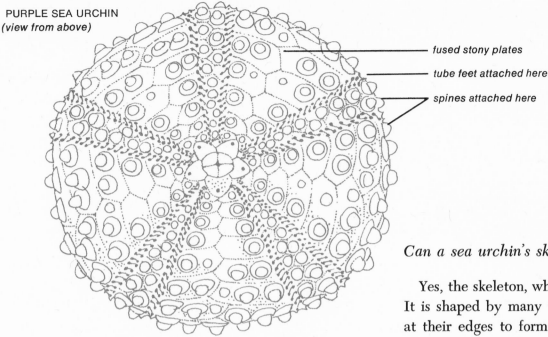

PURPLE SEA URCHIN
(view from above)

— *fused stony plates*

— *tube feet attached here*

spines attached here

Can a sea urchin's skeleton grow?

Yes, the skeleton, which is called a test, can grow. It is shaped by many thin pieces that join together at their edges to form a ball. The urchin grows as more stony material is added around the edges of these pieces. Each year, rings that look like the rings on the stump of a tree, are added to the skeleton.

Where do urchins come from?

Adult urchins cast eggs and sperm into the sea during the winter. Those cells that unite form tiny larvae that live a drifting life in the sea until they are ready to change into urchins and take up life near the shore.

Starfish

What can you see if you look at a starfish closely?

For a very close look at a starfish, it helps to have a pocket lens. On top of him, you may be able to spot the following: stony bumps and knobs, puffy water-filled sacks, a round stony strainer in the middle on top, and very, very small pincers between the bumps and knobs. At the end of each arm, you may also see a red dot.

All of these things have a purpose. The stony bumps and knobs give the soft body of the starfish a certain strength. The tiny claws pick up and toss back into the water any little pieces of rubbish that land on his arms. The stone plate on top strains and sterilizes water that comes into the starfish. It is im-

CROSS SECTION OF STARFISH ARM

fixed spines

skin gill

tube feet

movable spines

fixed spines

digestive gland

sieve plate
tentacle
eye spot

tube feet

portant for this water to be clean. The water the starfish takes in fills the little sacks or gills that poke up on the arms. These gills take oxygen from the sea water outside the starfish. The red spots sense light.

If you turn over the starfish, there is more to see on the bottom. In the middle is a hole that is the mouth. Inside it is a large thin stomach. Down the center of each arm is a groove protected by pale spines. Tube feet sprout along the groove by the hundreds. These are thin-skinned tubes with ends that have suction. They work on water pressure from the inside of the starfish. They use the water that comes in through the "sieve" plate on the top. The end of each arm also has a tentacle and tiny hairs for touching.

25

BASKET STARFISH

Does a starfish think?

A starfish doesn't have a brain like ours. He searches for food, eats, grows, and reproduces, but never thinks or feels. A starfish spends his life sensing things. He can tell up from down and light from dark. He senses wet and dry and can taste food in the water with special sense cells on his arms. A starfish also "knows" he cannot leave the water, much the way we know we cannot leave the air. When we take a bath or go swimming, we never try to breathe the water. We carry our air with us in gasps. A starfish can spend a few minutes out of the water, but as the water in him begins to dry up, and as he uses up the oxygen in the water, his life ebbs away.

What does a starfish like to eat?

Starfish like mussels and oysters best, but if they can't find those, clams will do. A starfish wraps his five arms around the shells and pulls until the shellfish opens up a crack. Some scientists think that the starfish injects something into the shellfish that relaxes it so that it loses its strength to close up. Others think the shells stay open because the animal is tired out from trying to stay closed. No one knows for sure. But once the shellfish has opened just a little, the starfish can begin to eat. A starfish has a small mouth, but a big, soft stomach. Food that is too large to go in through the mouth is digested outside. A starfish can turn his stomach out through his mouth and push it in between the shells of the tired shellfish. When the shellfish's body has been digested the starfish pulls his stomach and the digested shellfish back inside his own body.

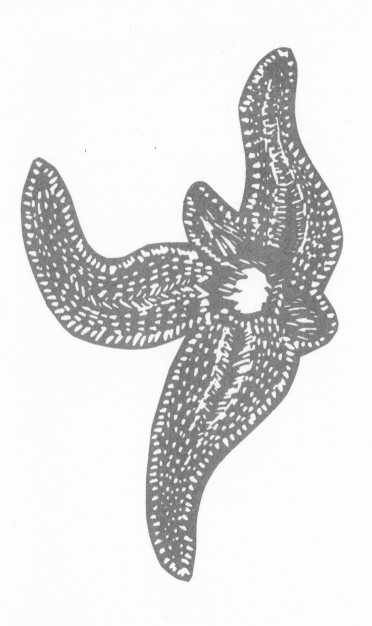

Why is one leg sometimes smaller than the others?

Even though they have hundreds of tube feet, and even though the tube feet are strong enough to open shellfish, starfish are not good at sticking to rocks. If a starfish is caught out in the waves he gets tossed and thrown against the rocks. Sometimes when he is hiding, he is injured by a falling rock. A starfish may lose one leg, and some of them lose half their bodies too. But for a starfish this is not always serious. A starfish can grow new legs to take the place of the lost ones. Sometimes a starfish grows a new half of himself. The new parts grow slowly until they look just like the pieces that were lost.

Do starfish take care of their young?

Most starfish never take care of their young. They simply shed eggs and sperm into the sea. The eggs that unite with sperm grow into larvae that must take care of themselves as best they can. Those that don't die or aren't eaten by other animals go through a complicated body change, called metamorphoses, and take up life on the shore.

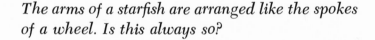

The arms of a starfish are arranged like the spokes of a wheel. Is this always so?

The only starfish that we see are adult starfish, and all of them are made like wheels. The arms all grow out of a central disk. This is true even for starfish with more than five arms. But, if we could see starfish when they are only larvae we would see a very different animal. A baby starfish has a right side and a left side, just as we do. To change from an animal with two sides into an animal shaped like a wheel is a very great change. This change is called a metamorphosis.

29

MOLLUSKS
bivalves

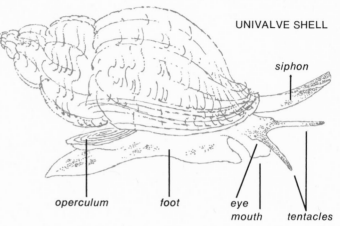

UNIVALVE SHELL

siphon

operculum   *foot*   *eye*
mouth   *tentacles*

There are many kinds of shells at the seashore. Are they alive?

Yes, some of the shells that you find in or very near the water hold a living soft-bodied animal called a mollusk. Of course you find mostly empty shells on the beach. They were once made by the living flesh of the animal, but now the soft parts are gone and just the hard shells lie drying on the beach.

Are mollusks all alike?

No, the soft parts of the animal are no more like one another than the shells are, and it is easy to see that there are many different kinds of shells. Some mollusks, like snails, have only one shell. Others, like clams and oysters, have two shells hinged together. Mollusks with two shells are called bivalves. Mollusks have a body, a stomach, and a mouth. Some mollusks have a head and some do not. Inside their bodies is a special mollusk heart.

32

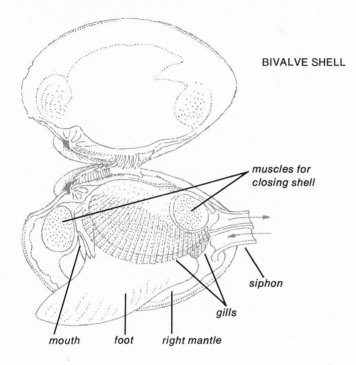

BIVALVE SHELL

muscles for
closing shell

siphon

gills

mouth   foot   right mantle

Where does the shell come from?

A tender skin, called the mantle, lies on the outside of the mollusk's soft body. This skin makes, shapes, and colors the shell. The mantle makes the shell larger as the mollusk grows.

What do mollusks eat?

Mollusks eat many different kinds of food. Some eat vegetables that they strain from sea water. Others scrape off plants from rocks. Still others are meat eaters and active hunters.

Clams

How do clams get under the sand?

Each clam has one foot. It is used for digging. By swelling up a little under the sand, a clam's foot can get a good, tight grip. Some clams hold themselves under the sand so securely that if you try to pull them out, their shells break. The razor clam is such an animal. But if you sprinkle a handful of salt over his hole instead of pulling, a razor clam will come up to get away from the salt. Then you can catch him.

A coquina clam follows the tide up and down the beach. It is carried by the water and uses its foot to flash down out of sight.

A surf clam has a fast-working foot and can dig away under the sand to escape his enemies.

Why does a clam hide under the sand?

If a clam did not hide under the sand, he would be tossed up on the beach by the surf. Only if he is buried can he be sure he will stay under the water. He also needs to stay hidden from birds, fish, and people.

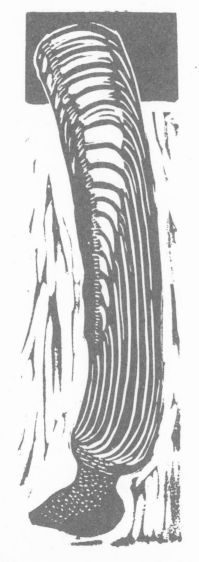

RAZOR CLAM

Clams have long, wrinkled necks that stick out of the sand. Why?

The end of their neck has a hole through which clams suck in water. Tiny pieces of food that come in with the water are sorted out by the gills and sent along to the mouth. (A clam's mouth is far away from his neck, and as for a head, it is just not there.) Unwanted food and wastes from digestion are blown out through another tube in the neck.

How many kinds of clams are there?

There are around eight hundred kinds of clams. This includes clams from all over the world, from warm oceans and cold oceans, from the Atlantic and the Pacific and the Indian ocean. Each kind of clam has a particular kind of shell. We have talked about clams from three of the most important clam groups: razor clams; coquina, or wedge, clams; and surf clams.

There is another group that is very large, called the venus clams. This is a hard-shelled clam with a purple edge inside. It is a kind of clam that people find very delicious. We often find bits of sanded-smooth purple shell on the beach.

COQUINA CLAMS

Oysters

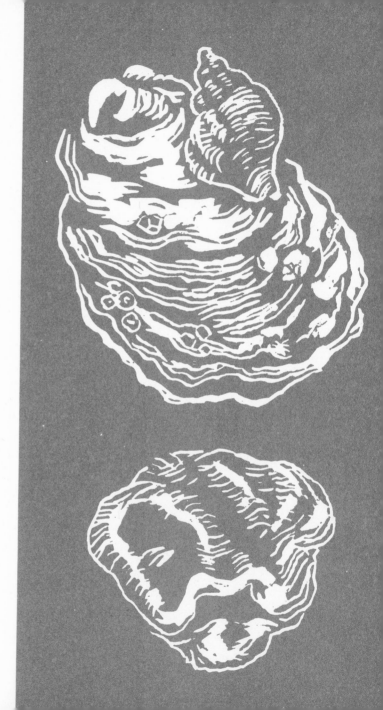

This shell is as wrinkled as the face of a troubled old man. What is it?

It is an oyster shell.

Is it wrinkled because it's old?

All the currents of the ocean waters and the dangers of life in the sea seem to be twisted into the oyster's crooked shell. And yet, for all its wrinkles, a three to four inch oyster is only about three years old. So it is not really an old man at all.

Does an oyster have many enemies?

An oyster is lucky if it lives even a day, because an oyster has so many enemies that prey on it from the time it is first formed. With so many oysters dying as infants and as adults, you may wonder why there are so many oysters in the sea. The reason is that every adult oyster lays millions of eggs or millions of sperm that unite in the sea into millions of infant oysters. If all of these millions lived, the sea would soon be jam-packed with oysters and there would be no room for any other animals. But while most of the millions die, some do live to grow into adult oysters and reproduce, and that is why there are so many oysters.

Do all oysters grow pearls?

Only "irritated" oysters make pearls. An oyster makes a pearl when a speck of sand or a bit of shell gets into the mantle skin. To protect itself, the mantle slowly builds layer upon layer of pearl around the troublesome speck. After a long time, the speck may become the round and shining ball that we call a pearl.

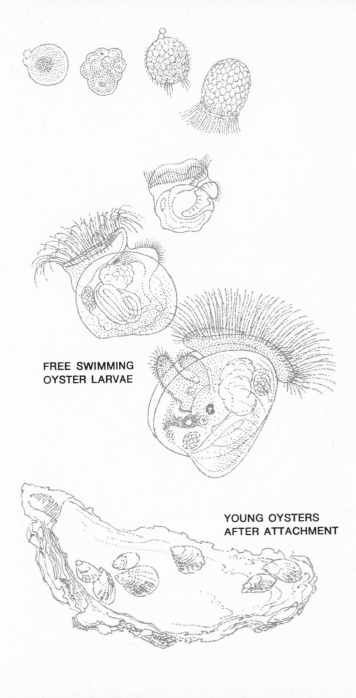

FREE SWIMMING
OYSTER LARVAE

YOUNG OYSTERS
AFTER ATTACHMENT

Scallops

Most fish stores sell white, marshmallow-shaped lumps called scallops. Could these lumps ever have been animals?

What fish stores call scallops are the muscles that once held together the two shells of a living animal. Each scallop gets along with one white muscle. By carefully arranging two flaps of skin at the edge of his shell, and by tightening this great white muscle, a scallop can jump, spin, roll, and swim through the sea.

Can a scallop tell up from down?

When a scallop lands with his flatter shell against the sea bottom, he knows it. So he jumps up and turns over. He likes his curved shell to be underneath him because it holds him up a bit higher. And a little above the sea floor the water is clearer.

38

Do scallops know one another?

We are certain that scallops do not make friends, but groups of scallops sometimes go traveling through the sea together.

A scallop can swim, but how does he know where he is going?

Although a scallop has no head, it has eyes and is the only bivalve that does. All along the edge of the mantle are more than twenty blue-green eyes. Each eye has a focusing lens, a retina, and a nerve. A scallop can see very well with all these eyes and can leap away from danger. No one knows what kind of sense a scallop makes out of what he sees, however, and it is strange that an animal with such marvelous eyes does not have much of a brain.

39

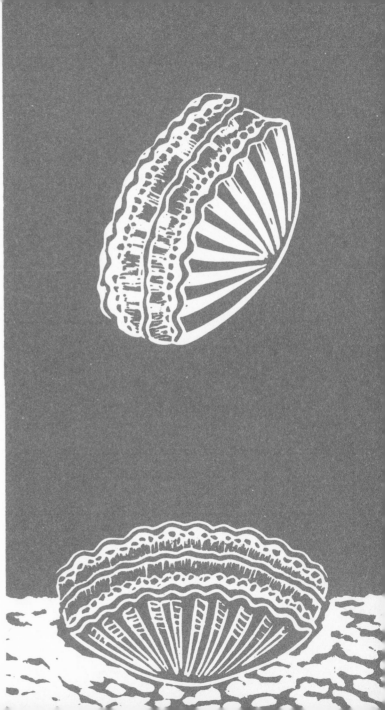

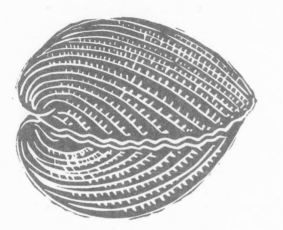

Cockles

Are all ribbed shells scallops?

There is another mollusk that has a deeply ribbed shell. The ribbing also starts near the hinge and ends at the other edge. But the shells are deeper, more dished out, than a scallop's shells, and the hinge is small and simple. There are no "wings," or "ears" of shell sticking out at each side of the hinge. These mollusks are called cockles. The two shells form a heart-shaped hiding place for the mollusk's soft body. Cockles live under the sand and send tubes up to the surface. Clean water holding bits of food is drawn down into the gills through one tube. Bits of food and sand that a cockle doesn't want are sent out in a stream of water through another tube. A cockle that is dug out of the sand can jump and spin. But it cannot swim away, and as soon as it is able to, it uses its foot to dig down under the sand again.

Jingle Shells

Delicate silver, orange, and gold shells blow lightly along the tide line on some beaches. What are they?

Jingle shells are as thin as leaves. Once they were attached to rocks under water. Then they spread their shells a bit apart to filter water through their tiny bodies. When you find an empty jingle shell, you will see that the flatter shell has a hole in it. This shell once had strong anchor cords coming through the hole to tie it to the rock. The cup-shaped shell lay on top.

Mussels

Sometimes the shore seems to be covered with blue-black shells. What are they?

They are mussels, which are bivalves that anchor themselves to rocks along the shore using special threads.

What will I see if I look inside a mussel?

If you open a mussel and lay back the mantle tissue that lies on top, you will see water going through the gills. At least six glassfuls, pushed and pulled by tiny hairs, go through a mussel every hour. The gills are sorting out food and they are also taking oxygen from the water. At one end you may be able to see the mouth guarded by two flaps of skin.

Why are there so many mussels?

Mussels are animals that face many dangers in life. They cannot protect themselves very well, so they reproduce in huge numbers. In this way, if some die, there will be others still alive. Mussels can neither shelter nor protect the eggs and sperm that they pour into the ocean. If the eggs and sperm chance to unite, they form growing baby mussels. These live as larvae in the water until they are ready for life near the shore. The mussels that you see clinging to the rocks are few compared to the number that once lived in the surf.

How old are mussels?

When the sea has plenty of food in it, and the animals at its edge are not too crowded, mussels grow about an inch a year. If you look closely, you will find some baby mussels hiding in empty barnacle shells, or growing up in cracks in the rocks. They can stay there until they grow too large and then they "walk" off on their only foot to find a better spot to live. Perhaps the next place they fasten onto will be a bunch of seaweed. Slowly, the two tiny shells will grow bluer and thicker until you can no longer look right through them. There is a good chance that a dog whelk or starfish will eat them, but if they live, they may be about an inch long at the end of the year.

How does a mussel travel about?

Each mussel has a walking foot to help it get about. The foot is long and narrow with a groove from one end to the other. When a mussel wants to attach itself to something, it pours a fluid down the groove. The fluid sticks to the rocks and hardens when the water touches it. The foot makes several anchor threads this way. When a mussel wants to go somewhere else, it breaks loose from the old threads and makes new threads in the direction it wants to go. It drags itself along. If you pick up some baby mussels and put them in a glass of sea water, they will drag themselves up the side of the glass on tiny anchor threads. The anchor threads hold them as they work their way higher and higher.

I see something soft and brown waving between the two shells. What is it?

When a mussel lies under water with its shells open, the edge of the mantle tissue sticks out between the shells. This is the skin that makes the shells larger by adding to their edges as the soft parts inside grow.

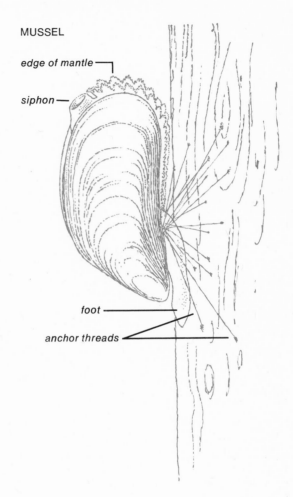

MUSSEL

edge of mantle

siphon

foot

anchor threads

MOLLUSKS
univalves

Limpets

What are these funny lumps on the rocks?

They are limpets, relatives of snails.

How can I get one up?

If you've let the limpet know that you're there, chances are good that you will break his shell before you get him off the rock. Then your only hope of seeing what lies under the lump is to find another limpet. Sneak up quietly and before he knows you are watching, give his shell a good hard kick. You may be able to knock him loose before he tightens his grip. Limpets have more gripping power than scientists can easily explain.

Why does a limpet need to grip so hard?

Not only is this gripping power a good protection against you and me and the birds, but it is also protection against the waves and the drying heat of the sun. When danger threatens, the limpet grips onto the rock, supplying himself with a little water to keep him alive until the coast is clear.

Can't water leak out from under the limpet's shell?

Most scientists seem to agree that when a limpet senses the turn of the tide, he stops eating and wanders back to a kind of "home." This "home base" is a groove that exactly fits the edge of the limpet's shell. Each limpet makes a groove, or home, for himself by rubbing his shell against a rock. If the rock is soft, it is worn away into the right-sized groove. If the rock is hard, the limpet's shell wears away until it matches the rock. With a good deal of patience, the limpet works to fit perfectly against the rock. Then water cannot leak out, nor can air leak in. When the tide is dropping, he finds his "home," pulls his shell down, and waits for the sea to come back.

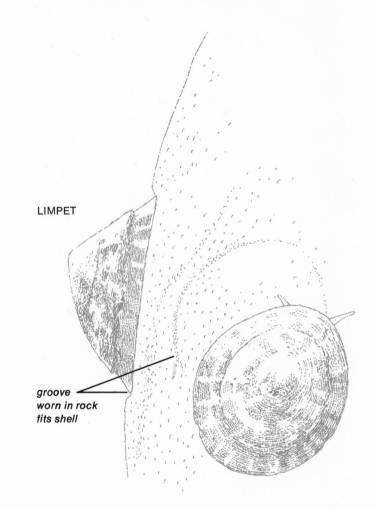

LIMPET

groove
worn in rock
fits shell

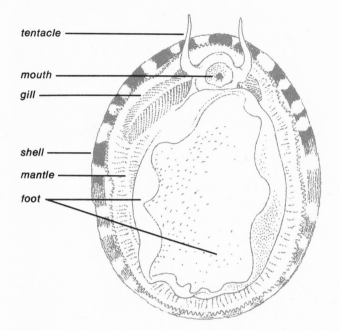

tentacle

mouth

gill

shell

mantle

foot

What do limpets eat?

They eat tiny plants called algae. A limpet scrapes off the algae from the rocks with a special kind of straplike tongue called a radula. The tongue is long and narrow. It is wrapped around a large muscle and has row after row of horny teeth embedded in it. The teeth are shaped like the teeth on a saw. When a limpet wants to eat, he rolls out his radula and the horny teeth scrape off algae from the rocks. When the radula is rolled back into the limpet's mouth, the algae are carried in also. If some of the teeth in front wear away they are replaced by teeth that grow in from behind.

It just happens that every scrape takes away a tiny bit of rock. It also goes into the limpet's stomach, mixed in among the plants. Year by year, the rocks get smaller and the tide pools deeper. All because of a limpet's radula and good appetite.

Some limpet shells are high and some are almost flat. Why?

A limpet's shell grows high if a limpet has to work hard to stick to a rock. If he lives in a tide pool, his shell is flatter. In a tide pool, a limpet does not have to fight the surf and air, and the shell is not pulled down so much by the muscles.

Dog Whelks

These snail shells look alike, but they come in different colors. Why?

These shells belong to dog whelks, sometimes called dogwinkles, a kind of meat-eating snail. The shell of the dog whelk is said to be colored by its diet. Some eat barnacles, and their shells are white. Others eat mussels, and their shells are black. A few have black and white stripes like a zebra, and scientists think that they have switched from a diet of barnacles to a diet of mussels. Still other dog whelks live in the heavy waves, and some of their thick shells are yellow, but no one seems to know why.

What is the long tube that sticks up above the dog whelk's head?

Thousands and thousands of years ago, dog whelks lived in places that had muddy or sandy bottoms. As they plowed through the mud looking for food, they stirred up the water. Dog whelks that had a long tube, or siphon, sticking up over their heads did not get muddy water in their gills. They pulled in clean water from up above, so their gills did not get clogged up with mud. Dog whelks born without siphons took in muddy water, and could not survive. When dog whelks moved onto the rocks to eat the shellfish and barnacles there, they took their siphons with them even though they were no longer needed. Having a siphon does a dog whelk no harm and no particular good, because the water is not muddy on the rocks. By accident a dog whelk may someday be born without a siphon. He will be able to live very well without it. He may even start a new line of dog whelks without siphons.

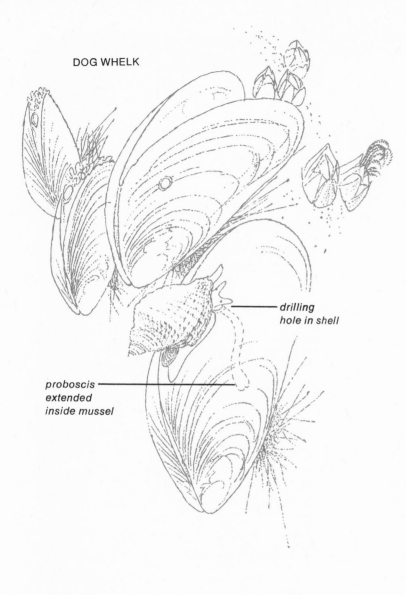

DOG WHELK

drilling
hole in shell

proboscis
extended
inside mussel

Can a baby dog whelk eat a grown-up mussel?

Baby dog whelks grow from fertile eggs laid in tiny wheat-colored capsules. A young dog whelk comes out of the capsule looking very much like his parents. But being so small, he needs to find food of the right size. So he starts off his life eating very small sea worms. When he's a little larger he moves on to eat small barnacles that are easy to open. And finally, if the supply of barnacles runs out, he learns to feast on young mussels. As an adult, he is at last ready to attack full-sized barnacles and any-sized mussels.

RADULA IN MOUTH
OF DOG WHELK *(carnivore)*

RADULA IN MOUTH
OF LIMPET

How does a dog whelk get inside a mussel shell?

The front end of a dog whelk's head is shaped into a long snout called a proboscis. At the very end of this proboscis is a slit of a mouth with a radula inside. A dog whelk's radula is very much like a limpet's radula except that there are fewer teeth in each row of the limpet's radula. A dog whelk can use his radula to scrape a hole right through the toughest mussel shell. Many young dog whelks have made mistakes and drilled holes in empty shells. But soon they learn to tell the empty shells from full ones. Once the hole is finished, the proboscis is pushed inside. The radula scrapes out the meat.

How does a dog whelk eat barnacles?

Barnacles can be forced open without drilling. That is why dog whelks like barnacles best. Only when the supply of barnacles runs out will dog whelks change to a diet of mussels.

Moon Snails

There are some bumps in the sand that move. What are they?

The bump you see moving along under the sand may be one of the boldest and the hungriest of the meat-eating snails, the moon snail. The bump is the snail's round shell, blindly plowing through the sand. A hood of flesh covers the snail's eyes and protects them from the harsh sand. The moon snail is searching for clams.

How does a moon snail get into a clam?

Moon snails come in two sizes, small and large. Small moon snails eat soft-shelled clams with long fat necks. The soft-shelled clam can't pull himself all the way into his shell, so he is easy to attack and eat. Large moon snails grow to a bigger size and they eat hard-shelled clams. The moon snail must drill a hole in the clam's shell to get inside. First he scrapes away the outer layers with his radula. Then with a special gland that makes sulfuric acid, which is a very strong acid, he melts a hole. The hole goes right through the clam shell. When the hole is made, the moon snail sticks his proboscis inside it and scrapes out the clam.

Does a radula take the place of teeth?

A moon snail has teeth down inside his stomach. His radula rips loose pieces of food that are sent down to his stomach to be chewed up by his teeth and digested.

Do baby moon snails live under the sand too?

Every moon snail is both male and female. All adult moon snails make eggs and protect them in sand collars. A sand collar is a sticky sheet of gelative that holds the eggs of the moon snail until they hatch. It is several inches wide, and might easily fit around a person's neck. Sand sticks to the outside of the collar when the moon snail leaves it half buried in sand under the sea. The eggs of one kind of moon snail (which is the large kind) hatch and swim away to live for a while in the tides. The fewer eggs of the moon snail (a kind that never gets very large) hatch, looking like tiny adults. They start to hunt for clams under the sand right away.

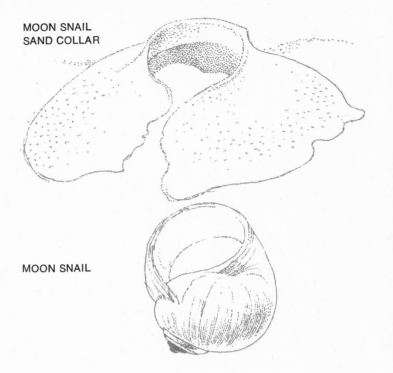

MOON SNAIL
SAND COLLAR

MOON SNAIL

Periwinkles

What are these crooked marbles, so ready to roll around on the rocks?

They are periwinkles, a vegetable-eating snail. When the tide is out, the periwinkle pulls himself completely into his shell and closes his trap door. A thin coating of mucus that he leaves on the edge of the shell glues him to the rock. But a gentle breeze, or the touch of a finger, will send the shell rolling down the rocks. If a periwinkle is tossed by the waves, his tough shell rolls and doesn't break.

58

Why does a periwinkle have a trap door?

The trap door is there to shut air out and shut water in. It is not a good defense against hungry sea gulls.

What does a periwinkle eat?

Periwinkles scrape tiny plants from the rocks with their sharp teeth. The teeth are not in jaws but roll out on the periwinkle's tongue.

59

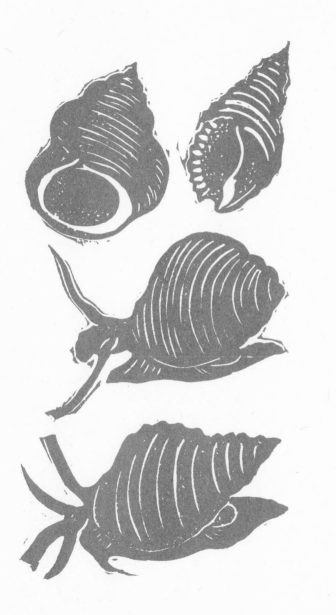

Can a periwinkle breathe air?

Most periwinkles get their oxygen from the water, but a few are learning to breathe air and live on land. The gills of these periwinkles are changing into a kind of air-breathing lung. But all periwinkles live in the sea when they are young.

What sort of a face does a periwinkle have?

A periwinkle has a kind of snout with two pairs of hollow tentacles and some simple eyes.

Can you tell a periwinkle from a dog whelk?

Dog whelks have ridges and grooves around the openings of their shells. Periwinkle shells have a smooth, round entrance. Periwinkles fit neatly into their shells, and can close themselves in snugly behind a round, trap door. Dog whelks try to hide inside their shells, but they seem too fat to fit. There is another difference that is easy to spot. Dog whelks have a groove that marks the place where its siphon reaches overhead. Periwinkles have no siphon and no groove.

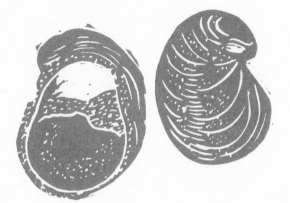

Slipper Snails

What are these brown and white shells that are shaped like little boats with a seat at one end? Did they ever creep about like other snails when they were alive?

Slipper snails are different from other snails because they don't move around. They stay in one place and live one on top of another, piggyback style. They sort out food from the water, which they draw in through their bodies, so they never need to go anywhere. The lowest snails in the stack are usually females, and the ones higher up are males. As they grow older, male slipper snails turn into females. In empty shells lying on the beach you often find young slipper snails.

PLANKTON

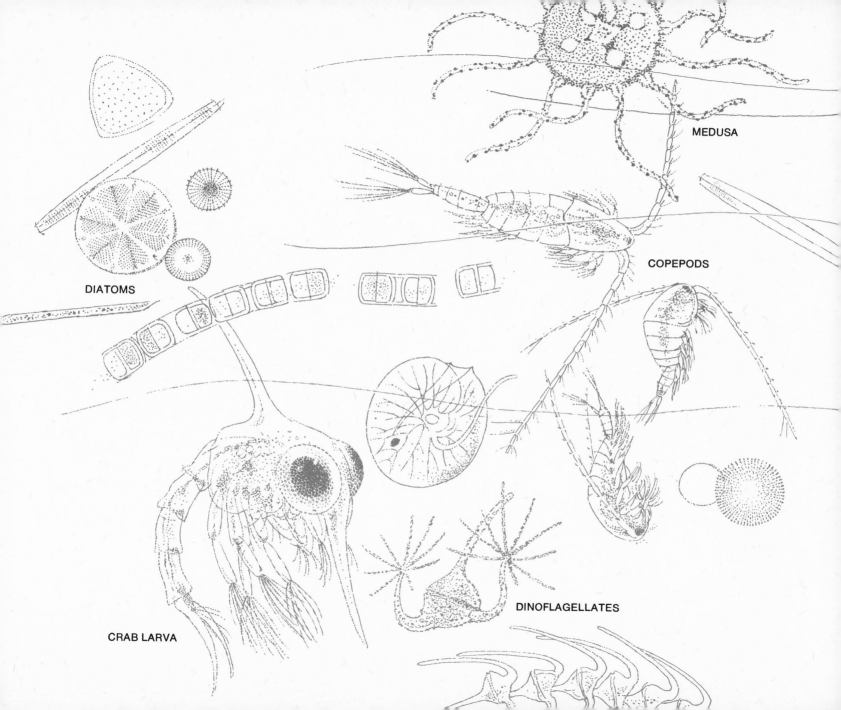

MEDUSA

COPEPODS

DIATOMS

DINOFLAGELLATES

CRAB LARVA

Plankton

What do oysters, clams, mussels, and other such animals find to eat in the clear sea water that flows around them?

Although the sea looks clear to us, it is actually filled with living plants and animals. We can see them through a microscope, but not with our eyes alone. Animals that cannot move around wait for the sea to bring these plants and animals to them for food. These tiny living things that drift around in the surface waters of the sea are called plankton. Plankton is as important a food for many seashore animals as grass is for cows. In an acre of sea water, there is as much "grass" as there is on an acre of land.

Plankton is made up of some plants and animals

64

ANIMAL PLANKTON

that *only* live a drifting life and of other plants and animals that live in plankton only while they are young. These temporary visitors finally take up life on the shore, if they have not been eaten while in the plankton.

Where does the plankton live?

It lives mostly in the first three feet of ocean water. Beyond this depth, the sun's rays become too dim, and the plants in the plankton cannot make "food."

What do plants and animals in the plankton eat?

Animals in the plankton eat the tiny plants and each other. The plants make their own food using nutrients from the water and the sun's energy.

SEAWEED AND SEA WORMS

Seaweed

The rocks are hidden by dark, drooping tangles called seaweeds. Are they like other plants?

As you watch seaweeds, they are quietly feeding and growing the same as any other plant. But seaweeds do not have a rigid stem to hold their branches and leaves towards the light. Instead, seaweeds are tough and rubbery because they must be able to bend and turn without breaking in the waves.

Are all seaweeds the same?

There are many kinds of seaweeds. Some are long and stringy. Others are flat or round. Some are bushy, some are smooth, and some are lumpy. Scientists divide seaweeds into three main groups: green, red, and brown.

Green weeds grow where there is a lot of sunlight. They are probably the ones you will notice first on a rocky shore. Sea lettuce lives in tide pools high on the shore. It is very green with wide leaves and curly edges. There are many kinds of green seaweeds.

Brown weeds live in deeper water. The sunlight is not quite so strong there. But brown seaweeds (and red ones too) contain green chlorophyll just the same. Even though the darker colors hide it, the plants are using it to combine the energy of the sun with nutrients from the sea to make food.

The chlorophyll in red weeds is also hidden by the color. Most red weeds live in deeper water than the brown. But there are a few that don't. One is especially easy to find in the tide pools on the shore. It is called corallina. Each part of it seems to be coated with a layer of lavender plaster. Corallina looks stiff, as though each section was jointed like the arms on a puppet.

How do seaweeds grow?

They grow from just above the holdfast. In this way a new plant can grow if the old one is torn away by the sea.

Do shore animals eat seaweeds?

Very few of the animals on the shore eat full-grown weeds. Some of the snails eat very young plants, and other animals hunt among the bits and pieces of broken weed caught among the rocks or in the bottom of tide pools.

What good are seaweeds?

Seaweeds are very important for shelter. They protect rock animals from the waves, from the heat of the sun, from the drying air, and from the freezing winter winds. Without the weeds many animals would be banged around and broken on the rocks, or tossed up on the shore to dry out and die.

Do seaweeds have roots?

Roots would be no use at all to a seaweed, because roots need soil to dig into. On the shore, the waves drive anything that is loose onto dry land. A seaweed can only live under water, so it clings to something that stands still. Since sand and pebbles shift around in the waves, rocks that do not move are best for seaweeds.

Seaweeds have holdfasts instead of roots. A holdfast is rather like a drop of melted wax that has spread out from the bottom of the plant and joined itself to a rock. The seaweed itself will break before the holdfast will pull away. Some holdfasts are simple, flat buttons. Others look more like the roots of a tree that twist and turn above the earth. The holdfast of oarweed, a brown seaweed that lives in deep water offshore, shelters many tiny animals in its hollows.

A sea plant takes its water and the nutrients it needs directly from the sea into its branches. The holdfast keeps the seaweed in the water and in a place where it gets enough light.

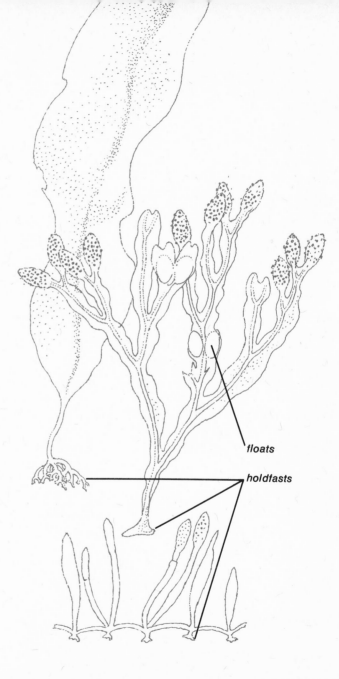

floats

holdfasts

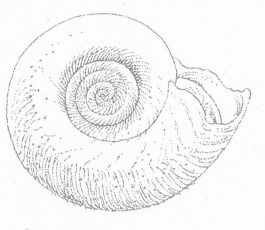

Spirorbis

Why are some seaweeds dotted with specks of plaster?

These specks are plaster tunnels made by a very small worm called spirorbis. Spirorbis builds his house on the rocking branches of the seaweeds so that he can fish in each new wave.

Where does he come from?

Spirorbis comes out of the sea as a tiny red-eyed larva. When he has begun his search for the right kind of seaweed, he has already been floating in the ocean for about an hour. Before that he has been protected in the egg case at the back end of his parent's tunnel. Once he is on his own, he is careful to choose a good spot for he will spend the rest of his life glued to the place he chooses.

— actual size

72

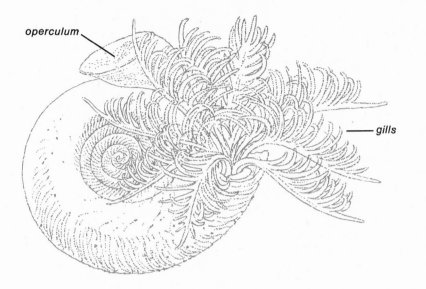

operculum

gills

What does such a small worm do?

Whenever the seaweed he lives on is covered with water, spirorbis goes fishing. He fishes from the end of his tube, using the feathery tentacles that are fastened to the top of his head. He fishes for plankton and oxygen.

When the tide drops and the seaweed is left in the air, spirorbis uses another, cup-shaped tentacle to plug himself up inside his house. The drop of water that he holds inside is enough to keep him alive until the sea comes back.

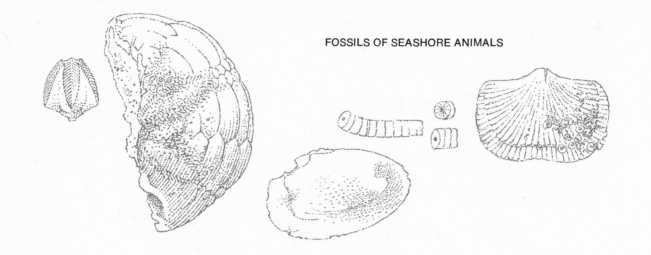

Can you ever see spirorbis fish?

Spirorbis will come a little way out of his tunnel to fish if you are very careful not to frighten him even with your shadow.

Is spirorbis very old?

No one seems to know for sure just how long each worm lives. But scientists know that for millions of years worms similar to spirorbis have lived in the sea. They have found fossil tubes of these worms in ancient rocks.

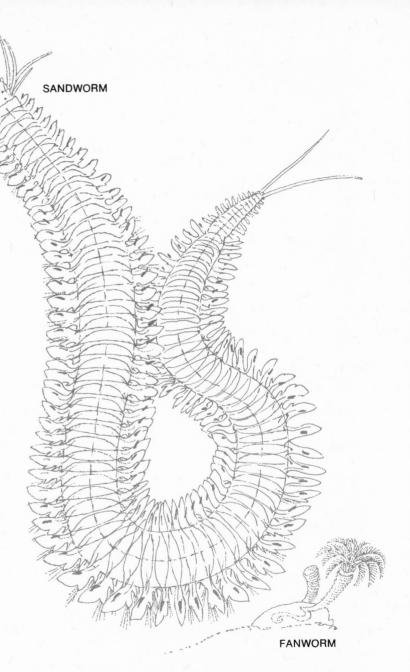

SANDWORM

FANWORM

Sea Worms

Are there worms on the shore?

Yes, there are many kinds of worms living in hiding on the shore. Some of them have smooth, slimy bodies with no divisions. Others have bodies that are divided into sections, or segments. The first few of these segments join together to make a head, and each segment has a set of bristles that serve as a kind of feet. These worms are scavengers. Using their eyes and tentacles, they find dead plants and animals and eat them with their powerful jaws.

Are they easy to find?

Most worms are not easy to find because they are always hiding, down under rocks, in deep rock cracks, in heaps of mud and seaweed, and in leathery tubes under the sand. But some worms build limey tubes and cement them down to rocks and seaweed.

JOINT-LEGGED ANIMALS

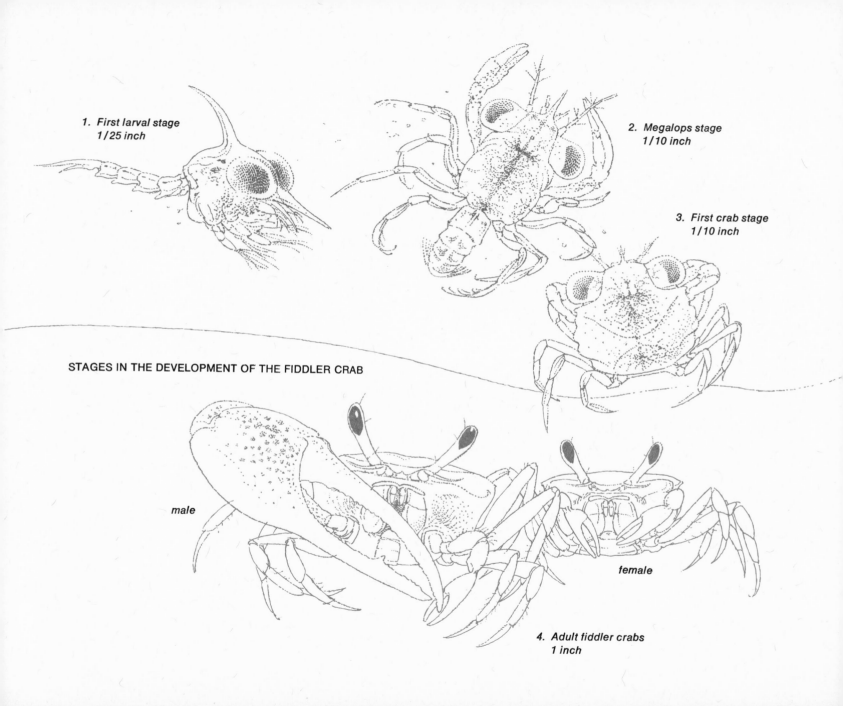

1. First larval stage
   1/25 inch

2. Megalops stage
   1/10 inch

3. First crab stage
   1/10 inch

STAGES IN THE DEVELOPMENT OF THE FIDDLER CRAB

male

female

4. Adult fiddler crabs
   1 inch

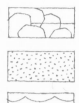

Joint-legged Animals

*Crabs and lobsters look very much
alike. Are they?*

Crabs and lobsters look alike because they are
close relatives. Both of them have bodies with three
sections: the head, the thorax, and the abdomen. In
both, the head and thorax are joined to form one
rigid section hidden under a stiff shell, the carapace.
Lobsters use their abdomen, which we call a tail,
for swimming. In crabs, the abdomen is much smaller
and is always turned under. All the soft parts of
lobsters and crabs are hidden. And both have five
pairs of jointed legs with special jobs to do. All
lobsters and most crabs live in the sea, and the young
of both grow up in the tides.

*What other animals have jointed legs
and stiff skins?*

There are many, many others. One close relative
of lobsters and crabs is the barnacle. But this is
clear only in its baby stages when it looks very much
like a crab.

Another similar animal is the horseshoe crab. But
although he lives in the sea and has a stiff skin and
jointed legs, he is not closely related to crabs. A
horseshoe crab has no true jaws, and his legs do the
chewing as he walks, so his closest relatives are the
spiders.

And there are still other similar animals, such as
insects, which, are not included in this book.

BLUE CRAB

Crabs

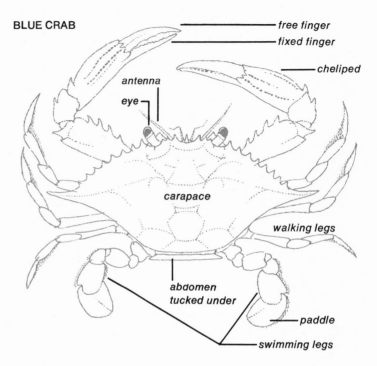

BLUE CRAB

free finger
fixed finger
cheliped
antenna
eye
carapace
walking legs
abdomen
tucked under
paddle
swimming legs

Are there many different kinds of crabs?

Yes, there are many kinds of true crabs, such as the fiddler crab, the spider crab, the green crab, and the hermit crab.

Then how can I tell if it's a crab?

If you can count ten jointed legs and can see a body that is wider than it is long, a kind of flap tucked under at the rear, two beady eyes on stalks, and a complicated mouth with a mean expression, then you can be sure you've found a crab. It is not always so easy to see all these parts. Some crabs hide their broad, stiff backs under heaps of seaweed or a sponge. Some hide half of themselves in empty snail shells. A few will swim away quickly through the sea, or dig backwards down into the sand. The legs can fool us too. Some crabs have long thin legs, while on others the legs are thick and strong. Some legs end in paddles, and others in spikes.

81

SPIDER CRAB

Why do crabs have so many differently shaped legs?

Every crab has the right kind of legs for its own kind of life. Crabs that swim have paddles on their back legs. Crabs that dig have a kind of shovel. Rock crabs have spikes that dig into weeds and grasp rocks when the waves are washing over them. And hermit crabs have special, dwarfed legs to hold to the inside of snail shells.

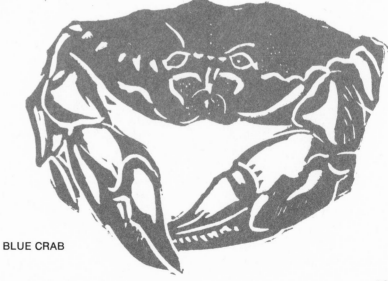

BLUE CRAB

What happens if you grab a crab by one leg?

If you grab a crab that way, he may twist around and pinch you. Or he might break off his own leg and run away. You will be left holding that one piece.

Why would a crab break off his own leg?

A crab does this as a kind of protection. When the waves cover the shore, it is not so peaceful on the rocks as when the sun is shining on them. Under the water, the seaweeds lash back and forth, and small rocks are being pushed around. Sometimes a crab's leg gets trapped under a moving rock. A crab could easily die of starvation in such a spot. But the third joint of every leg has a groove running around it that can easily break open. Without thinking about it, a crab can break off its own leg and leave it behind under a rock.

SPIDER CRAB

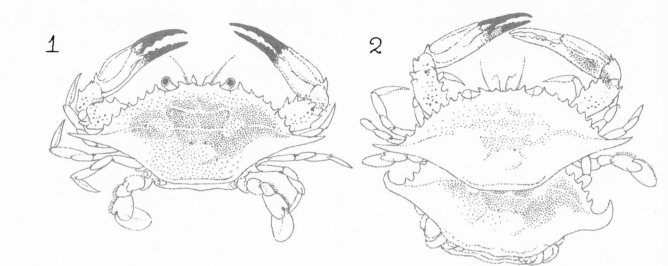

Can a crab grow a new leg? How?

A crab can grow back any leg he loses, including the claws he holds up in front. After a breakage, the open end of the third joint seals over so that the crab will not bleed to death. Then he must wait until his next molt. Crabs do not grow in the usual way for the outside of them is covered with a stiff coating. The soft parts inside grow until they are quite crowded underneath the stiff outer layer. When at last they must expand, the old small skeleton splits open, and the crab in his soft flesh walks away. After a time, a new skeleton hardens on the outside. Each time the crab exchanges his old shell for a new one, the missing leg appears a little longer and a little larger. Soon it is exactly like the lost leg.

Does it hurt a crab to shed its skeleton?

By the time the old skeleton is ready to be left behind, a new soft skeleton has formed under it. The nerves that once lay beneath the old crust now lie beneath the new one. It does not hurt a crab to step out of its old skeleton. In fact there is no reason to think that a crab feels things the way we do. For example, if a crab runs away we say it is afraid, because that is what we might do if we felt afraid. A crab has to get away from some things in order to live. It has to sometimes swim off, or dig down fast, or attack hard with its claws to protect itself. If a crab didn't do these things it might not last long. But even though it acts in a way we describe as angry or frightened, it does not mean a crab is "feeling" angry or

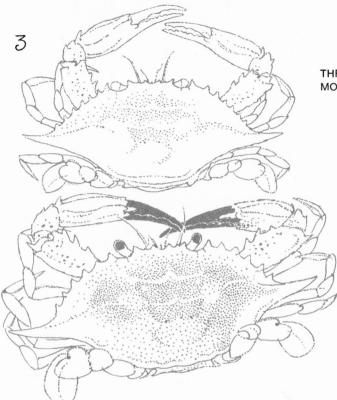

3

THREE STAGES IN
MOLTING OF THE BLUE CRAB

frightened. All we know about a crab is what it does. But despite the fact that it does not "feel" the way a human does, we can still respect a crab's right to live, and admire its strange and marvelous form.

How do crabs make babies?

Most crabs shed their eggs and sperm directly into the sea. These, if they join together, live through several changes of shape until, finally, they are ready to take up life on the shore. Hermit crabs carry their fertilized eggs on their stumpy back legs until the eggs hatch into tiny creatures that swim away in the plankton. They go through changes there similar to those of other crabs and finally settle down on the shore in a snail shell.

HERMIT CRAB

Do I see crab claws sticking out of a snail shell?

Yes, those are the claws of the hermit crab, who has lost the hard shell on his back and taken up life in a snail shell. Baby hermit crabs tuck their soft rear ends into tiny snail shells. As they grow, they move to larger and larger shells.

Why are they called hermit crabs?

Perhaps they were named after those lonely men who lived alone in caves in the mountains. The opening of the snail shell around the hermit crab is something like the entrance to a cave. But hermit crabs are not really hermits, for they almost never live alone. A small worm shares the right-hand side of the snail shell. The worm is protected and gets scraps of food. The hermit crab has a worm to keep the shell clean and move the water around inside. This kind of living together and helping each other is called symbiosis.

Sometimes, but rarely, an anemone lives on top of the hermit crab's snail shell. The crab drags its shell and the anemone as it goes along. The anemone has a broad base on the bottom of its tube-like body. The base hangs over the entrance of the snail shell making a larger protected space for the hermit crab to use. Then the hermit may not have to seek a larger snail shell quite as often. The anemone may be a kind of camouflage for the hermit, and may protect him with its stinging cells from hungry fish and birds. In exchange for these benefits the anemone gets the scraps left over from the crab's dinner.

Is it a crab that tickles my toes under the sand?

Under the sand at the edge of the waves live mole crabs. They look like small armored insects. They have strong paddle feet for digging. And the fine hairs of their antennae can comb even bacteria from the waves. We often feel mole crabs when our toes sink into the sand. Sometimes we find them when we are digging.

MOLE CRAB

87

Barnacles

Sometimes the rocks on the shore have a frosting of tiny sharp volcanoes. They cut my feet. What are they?

These are barnacles, some young, some old, some alive, some dead. They have each spent almost all their lives just where you find them. After floating in the plankton as a queer-looking baby, a barnacle leaves the waves and searches for a rock to grow on. When he finds a spot, he glues himself down and shapes stone walls about himself. He covers the hole on top with four trap doors. He will stay right there until he dies, not far from other barnacles.

How did barnacles learn to build forts?

Barnacles and other sea animals are never taught how to live their lives. A barnacle never "learns" how to build his fort. He simply "knows" how. This kind of inner knowledge is called instinct. Barnacles do what their natures direct them to do, without thought, and without choice. Other animals on the shore follow the commands of their own "inner voices."

89

Does a barnacle grow?

Barnacles are relatives of crabs and grow the way crabs do, by molting. When the soft parts inside have grown too big, a barnacle bursts out of his crusty old skeleton and kicks it off the tips of his six, bristling pairs of legs. The limestone fort is not cast off. It is made larger slowly, by taking away bits from the inside and adding more to the outside. No one seems to be sure when and how this is done.

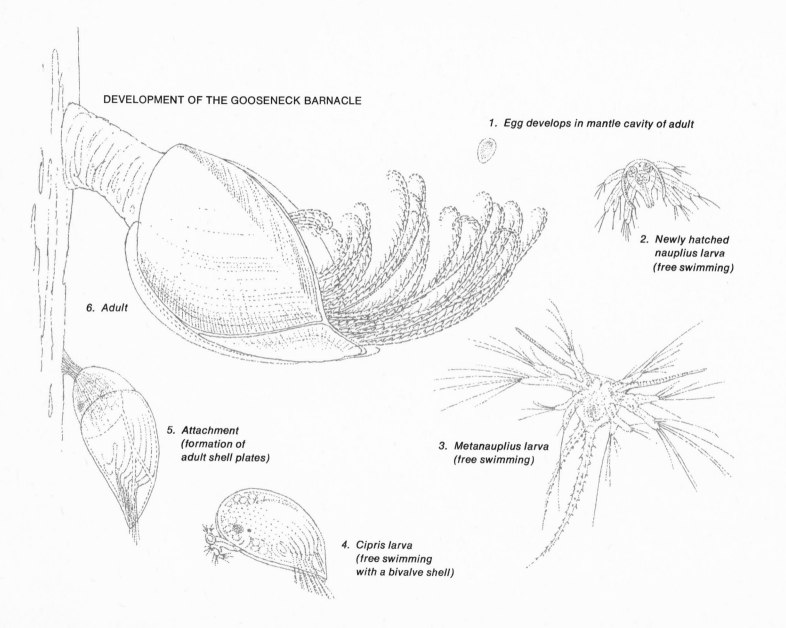

DEVELOPMENT OF THE GOOSENECK BARNACLE

1. Egg develops in mantle cavity of adult

2. Newly hatched nauplius larva (free swimming)

6. Adult

5. Attachment (formation of adult shell plates)

3. Metanauplius larva (free swimming)

4. Cipris larva (free swimming with a bivalve shell)

How do barnacles get food?

Barnacles get food by fishing for it with their feet. They sweep their hairy legs through the water, and when they have caught some food, they kick it down into their mouths.

What is a baby barnacle like?

A newly-made barnacle looks nothing like his parents. Once the eggs and sperm have joined, an animal is formed that looks rather like a crab. A young barnacle is sheltered inside his parent for four months before being sent out to live in the plankton. He goes through several changes in shape during his drifting life. Then something inside seems to say, "It's time . . . ," and the baby barnacle explores the rocks, then glues himself down head first.

Do the barnacles that grow on ships look the same as those on the rocks?

They may look the same or they may look even stranger, and be called goosenecked barnacles. The shell of a goosenecked barnacle is on the end of a wrinkled, leathery stem. If you look closely, you may find some barnacles growing on a piece of driftwood.

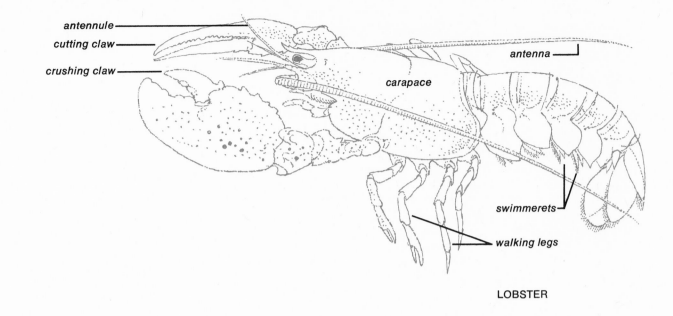

antennule

cutting claw

crushing claw

antenna

carapace

swimmerets

walking legs

LOBSTER

Lobsters

A lobster hides inside a horny skeleton. What is it made of? How can he grow?

The horny skeleton of the lobster is his outer layer of skin, or cuticle. It is made of a stuff called chitin, and it is stiffened by the addition of salts of lime. It protects the soft parts of his body, and gives them support. The muscles are hidden inside, and are used to move the lobsters legs and mouth and tail. A lobster's cuticle covers every part of him, including his eyes and down into his stomach. But it is not all equally thick. It is thin where it covers the eyes, and also in all the places that must bend. There is so little lime in it in those places that the cuticle feels somewhat like leather. A lobster must molt in order to grow, and he sheds every bit of the old skeleton, even all the way down into his stomach. The new skeleton takes a couple of weeks to harden.

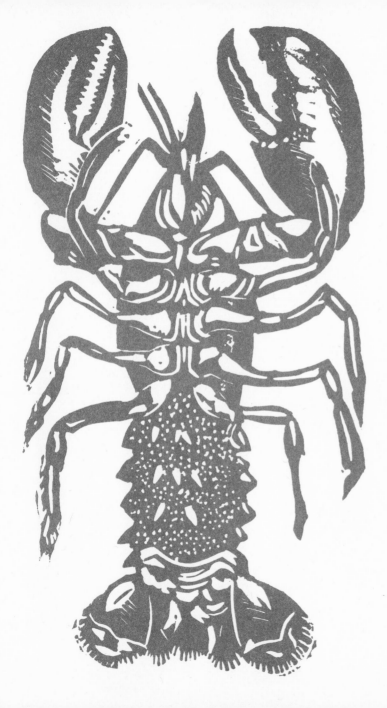

Both our hands look the same, but a lobster's claws are not the same. Why?

A lobster has one claw for crushing and the other for cutting. One is like a scissors, and the other is like a pair of pliers. A lobster has claws as tools to fix his food.

What are his back legs for?

Behind the giant claws are four pairs of legs. Two of them have pincers that can grab things, and all four pairs are used for walking. On a lobster's tail are a series of small paddles that hang down underneath. The movement of the paddles helps a lobster walk forward. The swimmerets, as these paddles are called, hold the eggs when they are laid. A lobster's legs also have more than one job. The part of the legs that we see does the walking. But another, hidden part reaches up under the armor on a lobster's back and holds the gills. The thin-skinned gills take oxygen from the water and pass it into the lobster's blood.

A lobster's strong tail helps him move too. By quickly swinging it down under his body, it makes him dash backwards.

Lobsters are always in fish markets. Where do fishermen find them?

They trap them in lobster pots in deep water offshore.

Do lobsters lay eggs, or give birth to baby lobsters?

Most of the animals on the shore release their eggs into the waves to develop. Lobsters also lay eggs, but they do not release them right away into the waves. Instead, they are glued to the swimmerets of the female lobster. The eggs are protected there and have fresh water around them all the time. But when the eggs hatch, the baby lobsters swim off to join the plankton. As they grow, they shed their cuticles. This happens several times, and they begin to look quite changed. Finally, they begin to look like lobsters and soon are ready for life near the shore, hunting clams and other food.

HORSESHOE CRABS

Horseshoe Crabs

Is this a dangerous beast?

Only clams and worms need to fear Limulus, the horseshoe crab, as he plows up the sand with the lower edge of his great shield. It's true that he is scary looking. It's true that he is one of the queerest looking animals that you will ever see. But there is nothing to fear. It doesn't matter if his closest relatives are spiders. Limulus has no poison sting and not a single vicious thought in his tiny brain. After all, what could his brain which lies in a thin circle around his mouth think?

Which end is which?

At first glance, the end with the long spine looks like the front end of Limulus. The spine looks rather like a sword, but it is the horseshoe crab's tail. He uses it as a tool. If Limulus is knocked over by the waves, he digs his tail spine into the sand and flips himself right-side up. Since the spine is the tail, then the round shield is the front. You can see Limulus's eyes on the top of the shield, one on each side and two in the middle.

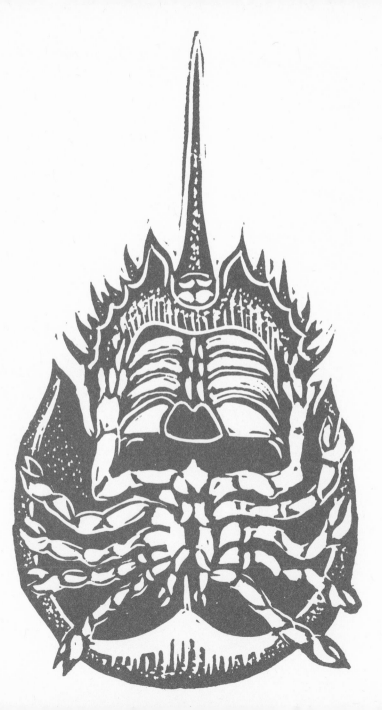

Sometimes we see two horseshoe crabs lying piggyback in the sand. What are they doing?

Probably the crab on the bottom is a female. She is busy laying eggs in a small hole in the sand. The horseshoe crab up on top is the male, and he is spreading his sperm over the eggs to fertilize them. In a month or so, young horseshoe crabs will hatch out. They will look just like their parents, but without tail spines.

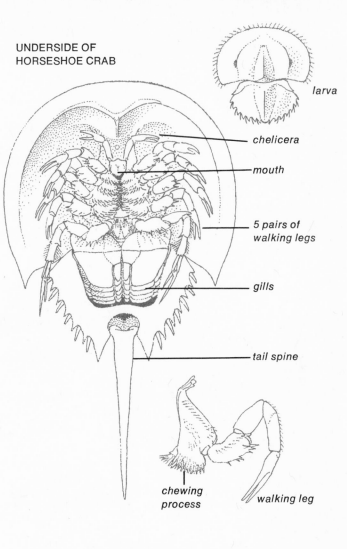

UNDERSIDE OF
HORSESHOE CRAB

larva

chelicera

mouth

5 pairs of
walking legs

gills

tail spine

chewing
process

walking leg

How does a horseshoe crab grow?

The soft parts of the horseshoe crab grow until
there is no room left in the shell to grow bigger.
Then the hard outer shell splits open and lets the
soft part of the growing crab step out. A new shell
is made on the outside by the soft body of the crab.

Where is the mouth?

The mouth of the horseshoe crab is on the bottom. It is surrounded by the legs. If you turn
Limulus over and look among his legs, you will see
his mouth, right where you would least expect it.
The legs have chewing parts around the mouth, and
as Limulus walks, he chews. In fact, he can't walk
without chewing or chew without walking.

101

What does a horseshoe crab do?

Limulus is best at just plain getting by. He sees poorly; he swims badly; and he can't defend himself at all. He can be frozen into the ice in New England and live through it, or be heated in the warm water of the tropical seas and not die. Limulus is good at living through things and always has been. Animals just like him have been on earth for 150 million years, and animals just a little different have been on earth for about 500 million years. Scientists have found fossils of the horseshoe crab in very ancient rocks. The horseshoe crab has been on earth since before the dinosaurs, since before the lobe-finned fish crept out on land, before mammals developed, for almost too long to imagine. During all the ages that Limulus has lived in the sea there have been many huge changes on earth. Mountains have grown, the ice ages have come and gone. Dinosaurs and some other groups of animals have existed and then disappeared. But the horseshoe crab has lived on and on.

JELLYFISH AND SEA ANEMONES

Jellyfish

Why do jellyfish smell when you find them on the beach?

When a jellyfish is stranded on the sunny beach, it dies and starts to decay. As this happens, it begins to smell. For although a jellyfish is 99 per cent water, a little bit is flesh. Flesh always smells as bacteria turn it into salts again. A jellyfish does not melt away into a sweet puddle that could be chilled back into shape again. It has been a living animal and once it is dead, the water leaves its body and very little is left.

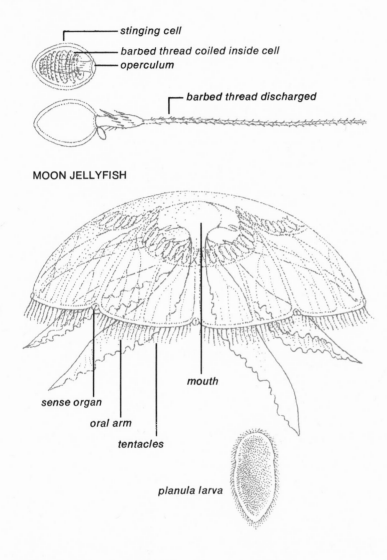

stinging cell

barbed thread coiled inside cell

operculum

barbed thread discharged

MOON JELLYFISH

sense organ

oral arm

tentacles

mouth

planula larva

People at the beach say, "Watch out! Jellyfish sting!" How do jellyfish do it?

All jellyfish have stinging cells that explode when they are touched. Out fly tiny poison darts. Jellyfish sting us only by accident. The stinging cells on their tentacles can make us feel miserable for a while, but there aren't enough of them on a small jellyfish to do us real harm. They were meant for tiny sea animals, not people. But there are some huge jellyfish that have a great number of tentacles and many, many very poisonous stinging cells. They are very dangerous to people.

What can you see in the jelly of the common jellyfish?

A jellyfish is made mostly of water, and you can look right into it. Inside you will see four lavender loops that lie next to four stomach pockets. The lavender loops make eggs or sperm. If the eggs of one jellyfish unite with the sperm of another jelly-fish in the sea, they form a planula larva.

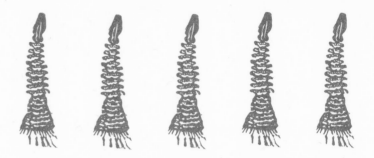

Does a planula larva become a jellyfish?

No, the planula larva itself does not become a jellyfish. The planula larva attaches itself to a rock somewhere. There it grows into an animal that looks like a plant. It grows and grows and as it gets a little larger, it keeps "budding off" new little plant-like animals like itself. Small pieces, or buds, shape themselves up so that they all look just alike. When winter comes, each of these tiny creatures divides up into a stack, like a pile of plates. The stack is joined together by muscles running up through the middle. Finally, the top "plate" on each stack pops loose and swims off into the sea. It is called an ephya larva. One after another, as spring comes, the animal "plates" pop off into the sea. They eat and grow and by the end of one summer, they have become full-grown jellyfish.

Does a jellyfish have eyes?

A jellyfish has no eyes or ears. But it can sense the light. Jellyfish can also tell up from down. In the sea, it is always swimming, trying to stay in the light near the surface of the water. Down below, there would be no food, and it would starve.

Four, long drooping lips surround the mouth of the jellyfish. The lips have tiny hairs on them. The hairs sweep water and food into the four stomach pockets inside. Living food is stung to death by stinging cells in the stomach. Then it is digested. For a common jellyfish, food consists of tiny animals in the plankton.

Why do jellyfish swim near the beach?

When we see jellyfish near the beach, it means that they are worn out from their one summer of life. They have been reproducing constantly and their strength has gone. They are so weak that the waves push them onto the beach. Still, until the end, they keep on pumping and eating.

Sea Anemones

What animal looks like a flower that is made out of flesh?

The anemone is an animal that is flower-shaped when it is feeding, and a brown, rubbery, polished lump when it is hiding. Anemones close up at the slightest touch. They sometimes close up when a dark shadow passes over them. On their tentacles are testing cells for getting signals from the water. If an anemone is alarmed, it folds its tentacles into its mouth and crouches down.

How is an anemone made?

An anemone is really nothing much more than a hollow tube, with an opening at one end. The wall of the tube has two layers, and in between the outside and the inside wall is a kind of jelly. The hollow in the center is divided up into many sections by thin walls, and when the tentacles capture food, they send it into this hollow. Food is digested partly in the space and partly inside the cells of the tube.

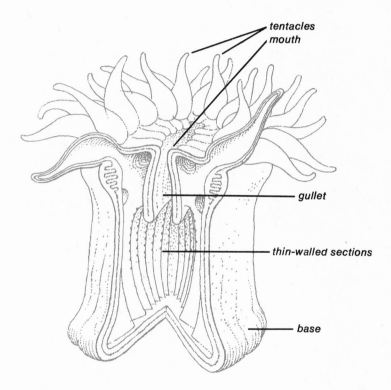

tentacles
mouth
gullet
thin-walled sections
base

What happens to the tentacles when they are inside an anemone's mouth?

Nothing more happens to the tentacles than happens to your finger if you suck on it. The hidden tentacles are safe from danger. When an anemone opens up, the tentacles come out and start to fish for food again. There are many kinds of anemones with many different kinds of tentacles. Some have thick ones and some have fluffy ones. The thick kind have stinging cells on them that are ready to dart out and kill small animals as they swim by. Fuzzy tentacles bundle up specks, and bending over, stick these specks through the mouth hole into the stomach.

SNAKE-LOCHS

What colors are anemones?

Anemones look like flowers not only because of their shape and tentacles. They also are beautifully colored. Some of them have dots and stripes. Anemones can be dark-red, brown, green, or orange. Some are red with green dots, others are red with blue dots. A kind that is pretty easy to find on the shore has a brown body and cream-colored tentacles. Some of the more beautiful ones are hard to find on the shore. But many aquariums have them in tanks where you can watch them.

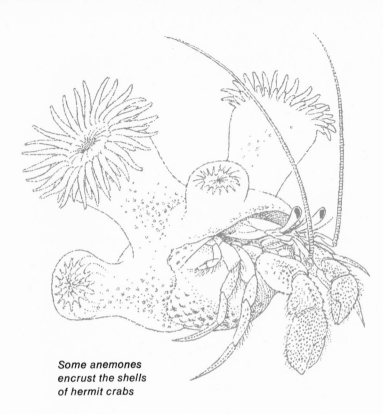

Some anemones
encrust the shells
of hermit crabs

Can an anemone move?

Anemones move from place to place by rippling the muscles on the bottom of the tube. They move slowly, often bending their tube bodies down and around as their tentacles search for food. Some anemones go hitch-hiking on the back of a crab, or on a hermit crab's snail-shell house. Others sometimes fasten themselves to the top of mussel shells. But most anemones stay hidden deep in shady cracks, or down in dark hidden places in a tide pool. Anemones try to stay out of the sunlight.

What does a stinging cell look like?

The stinging cell is a small dart with a coiled spring. The poison dart that can bury itself in the crusty outer layer of tiny sea animals. When the tip of the dart is touched, as it lies in the anemone's tentacle, it flies out of the body cell that made it. Sometimes it drags the whole cell right along with it.

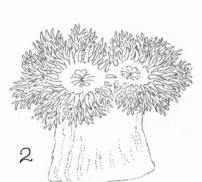

ANEMONE DIVIDING

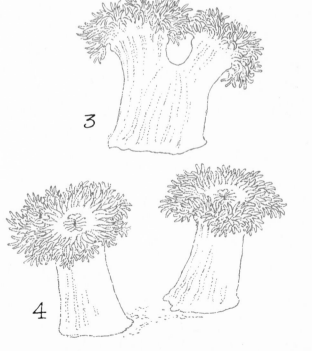

1

2

3

4

Do anemones grow old and die?

No one seems to be quite sure if anemones grow old, for they have many clever ways of dividing up into new young animals. Some anemones split in two by growing a ring of tentacles around the middle and then pulling apart. Some split in two from top to bottom. Where there had been only one animal there are now two. A Japanese anemone throws off its tentacles one by one, and each tentacle turns into a new animal. And still another kind walks away leaving small pieces behind as it goes. Each small piece shapes up into a whole new animal. With ways such as these to reproduce, it is hard to say if an anemone ever grows old. Each creature can make any number of new animals from the flesh of its own body. But while an anemone may not die of old age, it can die if it is left out of water, or if it starves.

115

SPONGES

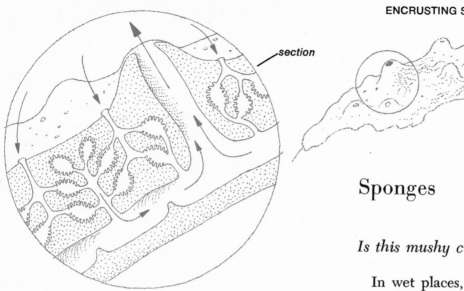

section

Sponges

Is this mushy crust alive or dead?

In wet places, hidden in deep, damp cracks, under seaweed, or in tide pools, you will sometimes find sponges. On a rocky shore, they look like a mushy crust, dotted with holes. But, whether they look it or not, they are living animals.

What sort of animal is it?

A sponge has no head, no eyes, no feet or legs, no arms or mouth. Instead it has an outside layer, and an inside layer. There is a thickness of jelly in between, and many tiny holes. These holes, or pores, bring water from the outside layer into the twisted tunnels made by the inside layer. As the water sweeps through the sponge, bits of food are swal-

118

lowed up by the cells lining the walls. The extra water and uneaten bits floating in it are pushed out through the holes. We can see the holes where the water comes out, but the pores that let it in are too small for our eyes.

Why do rock sponges grow so flat and messy?

Because the waves are always sweeping over them, sponges that live on a rocky shore lie low. When they are spread out thin, it is hard for the waves to break off pieces. A sponge under the waves cannot shape itself as neatly as a sponge that grows in deep, quiet water. A part that tries to grow tall can easily be torn away. So a sponge grows in any direction it can. But for all the "messy" look, each sponge arranges its cells into pores, tunnels, and holes through which water can flow.

Each cell in a sponge seems to "know" its proper place. A sponge can be squeezed through a piece of very fine cloth. Every cell can be torn away from every other cell. But in a dish of sea water all of the separate cells will group themselves together again to form a sponge.

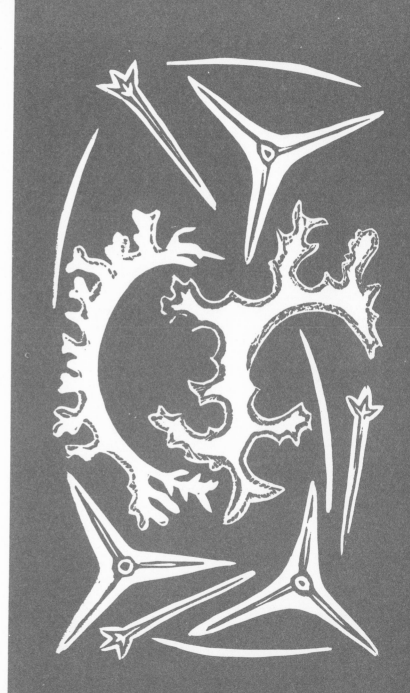

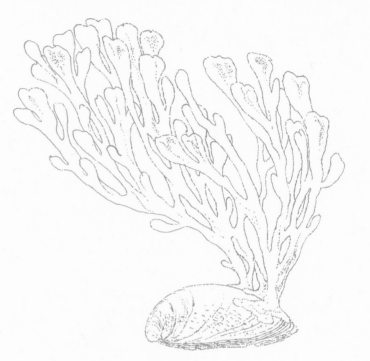

Some sponges are the color of plants. Why don't we call them plants?

Except for the most simple forms of life, those with only one cell, plants are very different from animals. Only plants can take the energy of the sun and use it to combine the salts in water into food needed for life and growth. Animals, including sponges, get their food directly from plants, or from animals that eat plants. If there were no plants to take the first step, animals would starve. They have no way themselves of turning simple chemicals into living body tissue.

What part of a sponge do we use?

If we are lucky enough to own a piece of real sponge instead of a piece of plastic shaped to look like a sponge, we own the skeleton of a dead animal. It is not a skeleton from a rock sponge, but from a sponge that lives in deep water and makes a supporting structure for its body out of a sub-

BATH SPONGE

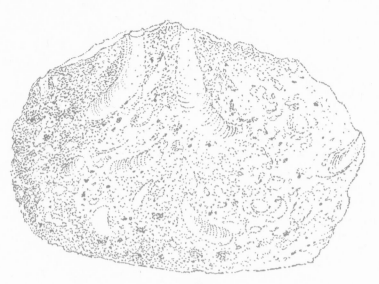

section

sponge larva

keratin skeleton

stance called spongin. Most sponges make some kind of stiffening rods for themselves. They are scattered here and there throughout the body of the sponge. But certain sponges in warm seas make a skeleton of keratin. By the time we see the sponge, all the soft flesh has been cleared away. Scientists separate sponges into different groups by examining the kinds of rods or skeletons they make to give their bodies strength.

Can a sponge grow old and die?

No one knows how old a crust of rock sponge is. Even as some parts of it are growing old, new parts are being shaped. It's hard to tell the old pieces from the new. A sponge makes more sponges by fertilized eggs or by tissue buds, called gemmules. A tissue bud is a small piece of the older sponge that shapes itself into a small lump. The lump can either swim away or stay where it is and grow into more sponge. So it is hard to talk about age when you are talking about sponges.

AFTERWORD

Most seashore animals live hidden lives. We find them mostly when the tide is out, at times when they are doing nothing but simply waiting. They do their hunting, fishing, and grazing at high tide. That is the very time when we cannot get near them so it's hard to learn their secrets.

Sometimes we are lucky, though, and we find some clams under the sand in the shallow water of the low-tide beach. Perhaps we see some crabs scurrying across the sand or some hermit crabs looking for their dinners. We may find some mussels hanging onto stones. Put the animals you find in a jar or pail of water and watch what they do. The clams may dig, the mussel walk, and the crabs try to escape.

A tide pool, which is a water-filled hollow on the rocky shore, is a good place to watch sea animals. Push the seaweed aside and lie quietly at the edge. You may be able to spot some barnacles kicking, and some snails grazing or hunting. Perhaps you will see a starfish looking for a mussel.

Take a little pad with you and make a drawing of the animals you find. Write down their sizes and colors and everything that you notice. Then you can take the drawing with you when you leave the shore, and leave the animal behind.

Explore the tide lines, where the waves leave tangles of seaweeds and shells along the beach. You will find the shells and egg cases of many animals that lead secret lives under the sand.